Painting on a CANVAS

9.95

Painting on a CANVAS

ART ADVENTURES FOR KIDS

CSCL

ANNIE WHEELER

Illustrations by Debra Spina Dixon

Gibbs Smith, Publisher
Salt Lake City

To Eric and Izzy, my creative soulmates,
and to my parents who gave me permission to create!

First Edition
09 08 07 06   5 4 3 2 1

Text © 2006 Annie Wheeler
Illustrations © 2006 Debra Dixon

Published by
Gibbs Smith, Publisher
PO Box 667
Layton, Utah 84041

Orders: 1.800.835.4993
www.gibbs-smith. com

Designed by Dawn Sokol
Printed and bound in Hong Kong

Library of Congress Cataloging in Publication Data
Wheeler, Annie.
  Painting on a cavas: art adventures for kids/Annie Wheeler ;
illustrations by Debra Spina Dixon.—1st ed.
    p.cm.
  ISBN 1-58685-839-4
  1. Art—Technique—Juvenile literature. 2. Art—Juvenile literature. I. Title.
N7433.W44 2006
701'.8—dc22

2006012171

CONTENTS

ART ADVENTURES

Art is awesome and should be explored by everyone! Art is not just fancy paintings in a museum. It helps you learn about the world by looking at things in new ways. Art also lets you express yourself through your imagination.

The art adventures in this book let you use your eyes and your hands to create wonderful works of art. Each project features a list of what supplies you'll need to get started. Read over the instructions before you start so

DO YOU WANT TO BE AN ARTIST WHEN YOU GROW UP?

There are many different ways to be an artist! A painter creates amazing paintings that end up in galleries and museums. A sculptor is another type of artist. As a sculptor, you could sculpt a famous basketball player out of clay! You could even become a muralist. A muralist is an artist who paints giant paintings on the outside of buildings, or even inside buildings or homes. You could also become an illustrator. An illustrator is a type of artist who draws pictures to go along with a story. Sculptor, painter, muralist, illustrator . . . there are many ways to grow up and be an artist. Just find your favorite!

you'll understand what happens next. Work at your own speed and ask an adult if you need help. It's OK to make mistakes, too. Some of the neatest art projects are made when something happens that isn't quite what you wanted. Usually, it turns out better. If not, try again!

The world of art has special words you can learn and use when you create these works of art. Try to learn those words and their definitions—they will help you understand different techniques and skills.

Finally, take the next step and add your own ideas to these projects. There is no right way to make art. Do the projects with a friend or family member. You'll be amazed at how different each project will be. More than anything, art is fun! Go ahead and start your art adventure today.

DARING TO DRAW

Drawing is simply taking a line for a walk. An entire picture can be created using just lines. Artists in Europe and North America draw mainly with charcoal, pencil, chalks, or pen and ink. Artists in Asia often use brushes and ink.

Meet An ARTIST!

During his lifetime, **M. C. Escher** created more than 2,000 drawings and sketches. He was born in the Netherlands, and decided to become an artist in his early twenties. He is best known for creating geometric drawings of strange buildings and interesting creatures. Some of the things he drew would be impossible in real life—lizards coming to life from paper, staircases that lead to nowhere—but that didn't stop him from showing the world how creative he was. Escher used his amazing imagination to draw simple objects in funny and interesting ways.

Contour Drawing

A *contour* is the outline of something curved or irregular. When you open a coloring book and see black lines on white paper, those are contour drawings. Contour drawings are fun to do because they're fast and kind of wild looking. When you do a contour drawing, look closely at the object you are drawing and quickly draw what you see! Remember, just draw the shapes you see, not the details.

What you need:

◆ Sketch paper
◆ Pencil or pen
◆ An object, like your shoe or a toy

Start your art adventure:

1. Draw the object with one long line. Don't look at your paper as you draw. Instead study the object.

2. Draw the shapes you see and the lines in the object. Do your best not to lift your pencil off the paper until your drawing is finished.

3. When your drawing is done, look at what you've created. It's a wild and beautiful contour drawing!

Blindfold Sketch

What you need:
- Sketch paper
- Pencil
- Blindfold, like a bandana, scarf or dish towel

Start your art adventure:

1. Sit down at a table and place the sketch paper directly in front of you.

2. Pick up your pencil and place your hand in the center of the paper.

3. Ask someone to blindfold you. No peeking!

4. Now try sketching your face from memory. Add details like your eyelashes, eyebrows, and the insides of your ears. Do the best you can and have fun.

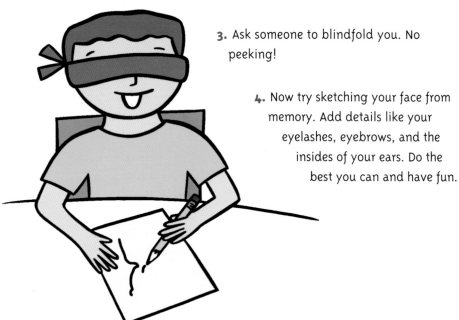

5. Take off your blindfold and look at your blind drawing. Does it look a little funny? Then it is perfect! A
blind drawing is not supposed to look exactly like
you. It is OK if one eye is at the top of the paper
and the other eye is at the bottom.

6. Try another blindfold sketch. This time think
of a place you really like to visit. Maybe it's a
beautiful lake, your friend's house, a rollercoaster
ride, or even your favorite park.

7. Once you've pictured it in your mind, close your eyes
and have someone blindfold you again.

8. Start drawing your favorite place very carefully. Think about where the
sky is in relation to the ground.

9. Take off your blindfold! Can you recognize your favorite place?

10. After you've finished both exercises, try doing them again, this time with
the blindfold off. You'd be amazed at how much better they look!

RIGHT BRAIN! GET YOUR RIGHT BRAIN HERE!

*This art exercise is a real workout for the right side of your brain. Why? Our
brains are divided into a right half and a left half. When you do math home-
work, organize your room, or do the dishes, then your left side of the brain is
working. When you draw, paint, or sculpt, then the right side gets a workout.
Using the right side of your brain will help you see things differently because
you use different thinking muscles!*

Through a Keyhole

What you need:
- ◆ Sketch paper
- ◆ Pencil and eraser

Start your art adventure:

1. Draw an oversized outline of a keyhole. The outline should stretch from the top of your paper down to the bottom.

2. Now, think about what you might see through a keyhole. Be creative. Maybe the keyhole looks into your bedroom. Maybe it's connected to a door on a spaceship. The keyhole might even open the door to a secret room full of hidden treasure.

3. Use your imagination to draw what you might see through the keyhole.

Radical Radial Designs

A *radial* design is one that goes out from a central point. In this activity, each section should look exactly the same as the others.

What you need:

- A plate that is at least 8 inches across
- Pencil and eraser
- Scissors
- Colored pencils, crayons, or markers
- Drawing paper
- Ruler
- Clear tape

Start your art adventure:

1. Think of a theme for your radical drawing, such as flowers, symbols, or geometric shapes.

2. Place the plate upside down on your paper and trace the outer edge.

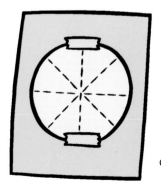

3. Carefully cut the circle out. If you need help, ask an adult.

4. Fold the circle in half, then in quarters, then in eighths. Unfold and smooth out the circle. To hold the circle in place you may need to tape it onto a larger piece of paper.

5. Draw the first shape in the center of your circle. If your shape is a flower then you would draw the center of the flower in the center of your circle. Next you would add the petals, one in each section. Carefully connect them to the flower center.

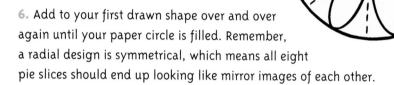

6. Add to your first drawn shape over and over again until your paper circle is filled. Remember, a radial design is symmetrical, which means all eight pie slices should end up looking like mirror images of each other.

7. When you have finished, hang your radical radial design from the ceiling or in front of a window!

RADIAL DESIGNS
Symmetrical objects appear all around you. Here are some other ideas to try:

Sun

Star

Spider web

Snowflake

Leaf

PAINTING PLEASURES

Thousands of years ago, artists created images of what they saw around them. These first artists painted beautiful pictures in caves and on rocks. Today, artists don't have to crush the petals of a flower to mix into paint, like those long-ago artists. We can choose from watercolors, oils, acrylics, and more. Like our ancestors, we should paint beautiful and mysterious pictures and hang them around us!

Meet An ARTIST!

Vincent Van Gogh taught himself how to paint and created more than 800 oil paintings. Although he only sold one of his paintings during his lifetime, today his paintings sell for millions of dollars. He was one of the first painters to paint things in colors that actually weren't there, like a green cloud or a purple horse. Van Gogh could show whether he was happy, sad, or frustrated through the way he painted. One of his most famous paintings is called "Starry Starry Night." It shows the blue night sky full of stars and planets that look like rockets of burning yellow. The painting seems to move when you look at it. What do you think Van Gogh was feeling when he painted it?

Van Gogh's Sky

What you need

- Oil paints and brushes, oil pastels, or crayons
- Canvas (if using oil paints) or sketch paper
- A photograph or magazine picture of the sky, either day or night, (you can also paint while looking out a window)
- Pencil and eraser

Start your art adventure

1. First, think about what kind of emotion you want to show through your painting. Happy? Angry? Sad? Excited? Frustrated? Loving?

2. Sketch the sky. You can also draw some land, rooftops, or treetops in your picture, but remember to make most of your picture about the sky.

3. Paint your sky according to the emotion you chose. Try to use colors, lines, and textures that will bring that feeling out.

Remember, Van Gogh used intense, beautiful colors in his paintings that weren't necessarily found in the sky. You can do this too! For example, instead of filling in a cloud with plain white paint, use swirls of light grey, white, and lavender. Use your imagination.

4. When your painting is finished, ask someone if they can guess what emotion you were trying to paint.

FEELING BLUE? COLOR YOUR EMOTIONS!

Artists express different emotions by using various colors and sizes of lines. Bright colors and thick lines evoke happy feelings. Sad feelings are shown by darker colors like blue, gray, or purple. Wild lines and sharp angles create excitement. Soft, round shapes create calm feelings.

Supersized

What you need:

- ◆ Acrylic paint or craft paint
- ◆ Thick paper or painting canvas at least 10" x 12"
- ◆ Pencil and eraser
- ◆ Clear tape
- ◆ An interesting object smaller than the size of your fist

Start your art adventure:

1. Set your interesting object in front of your drawing space where you can easily see it.

2. Draw your object, but instead of drawing its real size, SUPERSIZE IT! Try drawing it at least four times bigger than it is. It's okay if the sketch of your object is so big it goes off the sides of the paper. That will make the drawing more interesting.

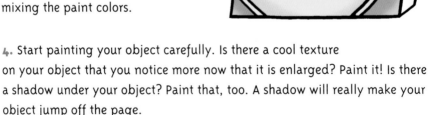

3. When your drawing is finished, start mixing the paint colors.

4. Start painting your object carefully. Is there a cool texture on your object that you notice more now that it is enlarged? Paint it! Is there a shadow under your object? Paint that, too. A shadow will really make your object jump off the page.

5. Let your painting dry. Later, show it to a few people and see if they can guess what you've SUPERSIZED!

Texture Impressions

Texture is all around us. The rough feel of sandpaper, the bumpiness of a wicker basket, the softness of a feather, these are all textures we experience everyday. Now you can capture the texture of everyday objects forever on paper!

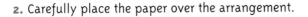

What you need:
- Found objects from home or nature that have an interesting texture. Items could include coins, leaves, keys, shoelaces, etc.
- Pastels or chalk
- Thin plain white paper

Start your art adventure:

1. Arrange a few of the objects on a table. Make sure your arrangement is smaller than the size of your paper.

2. Carefully place the paper over the arrangement.

3. With the flat side of your chalk or pastel, gently rub over the covered objects until their texture appears on the paper. You can change the color of pastel or chalk as you go.

CEMETERY RUBBINGS

You and an adult could take a trip to the local cemetery and do a rubbing of a headstone. Choose headstones that either have a special meaning to you or ones that have interesting textures or pictures on them. Make sure to bring a big sheet of white butcher paper, scissors, and the biggest piece of black chalk or art charcoal you can find. Take care not to disturb anything in the cemetery. Treat each headstone with respect.

4. When you are finished, take your drawings around and have people try to guess what each object is.

RUBBINGS

Do you love drawing castles but hate drawing all those tiny bricks on the outside? Why not use texture rubbing to help make the stone on your castle drawing? First, draw an outline for your castle. Next, place your paper on top of cement, a brick, or stucco surface. Start rubbing only inside the sketch you've drawn. Doesn't your castle look rough and realistic?

Silhouette Wet into Wet

Wet into wet is a wonderful watercolor technique that is easy and fun to do. When you use a **wet** paintbrush to paint onto a **wet** piece of paper it's called wet into wet. Use this technique to paint a beautiful sunset behind a landscape in silhouette. A *silhouette* is an outline of something filled in with a solid color.

What you need:

- Watercolor paints and water
- Watercolor paper or white paper
- Water dish
- 1 large and 1 small paintbrush
- Black crayon or marker

Start your art adventure:

1. Lightly sketch a landscape on your paper. A landscape is a picture that shows nature. Your landscape could include trees, brushes, grass, or the ocean. You can decide!

2. Dip the large brush in clean water and wet the whole paper.

3. Wet the watercolor paints in order to get them moist enough to use. You can choose any colors that resemble sunset, like pink, orange, or lavender.

4. Brush the wet paint onto the wet paper in a long sweeping motion across the entire page. Rinse your brush quickly and dip your small brush into the next color.

5. Brush the new color above or below your previous color. Use a lot of different pastel colors to make your sunset soft and beautiful.

6. Stop and look at your painting. Are the colors too dark? If so try adding more water to your brush. Also make sure your paper is still wet before you paint on top of it.

6. After your watercolor dries completely (this may take up to an hour), sketch in a landscape in silhouette.

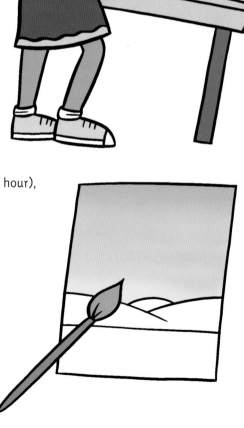

7. Fill in the landscape with black crayon or oil pastel. The finished painting should look like a real sunset. Now you are a wet-into-wet painting pro!

SILHOUETTE PROFILE

You will need black construction paper and a piece of white chalk, colored pencil, or crayon for this project. Sit side by side a parent or friend. Each of you should have a piece of black paper in front of you. One of you will go first and draw the other's face in profile. Just a simple outline. As soon as you have both finished, cut out the profiles you've drawn and hang them on a wall. See if people can guess who is who from your black silhouettes!

Straw Painting

What you need:

◆ Newspaper
◆ Removable tape
◆ Drawing paper
◆ Poster paints
◆ Plastic drinking straw

Start your art adventure:

1. Cover the work surface with newspaper.

2. Place drawing paper in the center of the newspaper and tape it down.

3. Add a small amount of water to the poster paint and mix together. Place one of the colors of paint on the paper.

4. Using your straw, blow the paint around on the paper.

5. Before the first paint color dries, add another color. Let the paint overlap as you blow to see what interesting colors are made.

6. After the paint has completely dried, show off your straw art. See if anyone can guess what object you used to paint with.

MYSTERIOUS MASKS

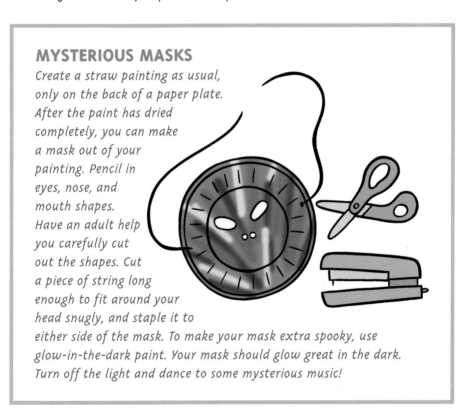

Create a straw painting as usual, only on the back of a paper plate. After the paint has dried completely, you can make a mask out of your painting. Pencil in eyes, nose, and mouth shapes. Have an adult help you carefully cut out the shapes. Cut a piece of string long enough to fit around your head snugly, and staple it to either side of the mask. To make your mask extra spooky, use glow-in-the-dark paint. Your mask should glow great in the dark. Turn off the light and dance to some mysterious music!

PAPER ART

Paper is all around. We use it to decorate walls, wrap presents, clean up messes and write on it. Many artists use paper to draw on, but did you know that paper itself can become art? Paper of all kinds can be used to create unique and lasting art projects. Instead of using new paper for this project, try to find a way to recycle old paper. You can use old magazines, newspaper, wrapping paper, cereal boxes, junk mail, and more. By turning the old paper into something beautiful, you'll also be helping the environment!

Meet An ARTIST!

Henri Matisse was born in 1869 in France. He was a lawyer before he became a painter at the age of 21. As an artist, Matisse brought new ideas into art culture. He used color in a fresh and different way. Matisse's art was soon being shown in museums around the world. Matisse invented a new form of art that he called "drawing with scissors." Before long, he was cutting out hundreds of shapes from colorful sheets of paper—curvy, large, zigzag, and even letters. He would cover the walls in his home with wonderful paper creations. Even when Matisse grew old and had to stay in a wheelchair, he created art.

Tissue Paper Bouquet

- Tissue paper, various colors
- Pipe cleaners
- Scissors
- Floral wire
- Paper
- Ruler
- Clear tape

Start your art adventure:

1. Cut colored tissue paper into flowers of three different shapes, including small, medium and large. Make the shapes of your flowers different—curvy, pointy, and in-between.

2. Stack your flower shapes with a large piece on the bottom, medium shape in the middle, and a small one on top. Use contrasting colors to create bright flowers.

3. Have an adult help you poke a pipe cleaner through the center of the flower shapes. Enter underneath the stack and thread your pipe cleaner up and through until about three inches are above the stack of flower shapes.

4. Now thread the pipe cleaner back down the flowers center as close to the original hole as you can.

5. Wrap the excess pipe cleaner around itself tightly. Some pipe cleaners have a sharp edge. Use a piece of tape to wrap around the top part of the stem to make it easier to hold.

Create a lot of flowers and use them for different projects!

Make a bouquet for a vase

Use a few to decorate a birthday present

Bend the pipe cleaners in a circle and use them as napkin holders

Link them together to form a flower chain

ART AND CULTURE

Tissue paper flowers are also called Cinco De Mayo flowers in Mexico. Cinco De Mayo means the fifth of May. It is an important holiday in Mexico because it marks the victory of the Mexican army in a big battle. There are parades, mariachi music, dancing, and decorations of special tissue paper flowers. This is a great example of art being a big part of tradition.

The Magic of Mosaics

A *mosaic* is a picture made by setting small colored pieces of paper, stone, or tile onto a strong surface, like paper, cardboard, or even a floor.

What you need:

- ◆ Multicolored construction paper
- ◆ Egg carton
- ◆ Glue stick with glue that dries clear
- ◆ Scissors
- ◆ Pencil and eraser
- ◆ Drawing paper

Start your art adventure:

1. Sketch a simple picture onto a piece of black construction paper. (Dark blue or purple paper will also work.)

2. Decide what other colors you want in your picture and cut out colored paper

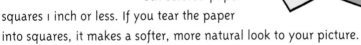

squares 1 inch or less. If you tear the paper into squares, it makes a softer, more natural look to your picture.

3. You may wish to use an egg carton to separate and save your multi-colored pieces of paper.

4. Fill in your drawing by gluing down pieces of colored paper squares.

5. Try to place dark colors next to light colors for high contrast. Take a step back from time to time as you work, notice how different the picture looks as you step away from the picture and the squares get smaller.

STEPPING STONE MOSAIC

Why not try making a pebble mosaic? You can make a simple mosaic just with black and white pebbles, which you can get at any gardening store. Sketch out a cool pattern idea and then set your stones in plaster of paris, or in cement while following your sketch. Place your cool mosaic in the garden or as the centerpiece for a table.

Magazine Beads

What you need:

- Old magazines
- Cup with 3 tablespoons of water in it
- White glue
- Paintbrush for glue
- String or yarn
- Plastic coffee stirrer or straw

Start your art adventure:

1. Look through the magazines and tear out colorful, interesting pages. These pages will eventually turn into your beads.

2. Cut out long triangles from the chosen magazine pages, about 5 inches long and 2 inches wide.

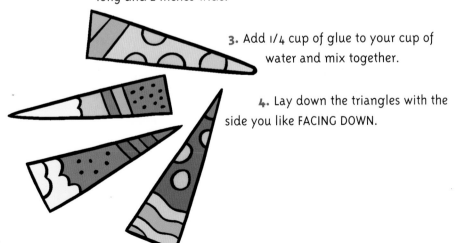

3. Add 1/4 cup of glue to your cup of water and mix together.

4. Lay down the triangles with the side you like FACING DOWN.

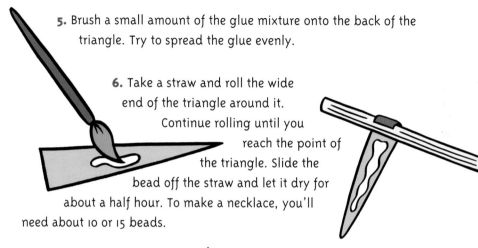

5. Brush a small amount of the glue mixture onto the back of the triangle. Try to spread the glue evenly.

6. Take a straw and roll the wide end of the triangle around it. Continue rolling until you reach the point of the triangle. Slide the bead off the straw and let it dry for about a half hour. To make a necklace, you'll need about 10 or 15 beads.

7. After all of your beads have dried, string them togeth-er. Remember to tie the ends of your string in a double knot so that it won't come loose.

SPELL IT OUT
Try cutting triangles out of magazine pages that only have words on them. Roll your triangle up so the words face outwards. See if you can make a sentence out of your magazine beads. Line them up on the string so that your sentence can be read by people.

Positively Negative

What you need:
- Assortment of colored paper, including black
- Scissors
- Pencil
- Glue
- String
- Clear tape
- White chalk or pastel

Start your art adventure:

I. Choose your favorite color of paper and fold it in half.

2. Pencil in a design on the fold. Your design could be geometric, curved or a combination of both.

3. Cut the shape out carefully, then open it up and glue it onto a black piece of paper.

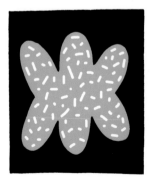
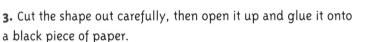

4. The shape is called the positive space and the space around it on the black paper is called negative space.

Positive shape   Negative shape

5. Fill in the negative space with a fun design using your white chalk or pastel.

6. Cut a fancy border around the black paper.

7. Tape the string to the back of the paper and hang your creation in a window or from your ceiling. You'll never feel negative when you see it. In fact, it'll make you feel positively happy that you are becoming such a great artist.

Stained Glass Window

Have you ever seen a stained glass window inside a church or an old house? The way the light shines through the colored glass is beautiful. You can capture this beauty using black paper, glue, and tissue paper!

What you need:

◆ Black construction paper
◆ Multi-colored tissue paper
◆ White glue or glue stick
◆ Scissors
◆ String
◆ White colored pencil or crayon

Start your art adventure:

1. Draw a simple design on a black piece of paper with a white colored pencil or white crayon. The design should be made up of blocks of shapes. For example, if

your design were to be a flower it should be drawn simply.

2. Cut out the shapes, leaving a thick black border between them. You will fill the shapes in with torn tissue paper.

3. Choose your colors of tissue paper, and tear them into large squares.

4. Spread glue onto a small area on the back of your design. Press the tissue paper onto the glue. Overlap with different shades of the same color.

5. Repeat this process until your whole design is covered with tissue paper.

6. The backside of the paper won't look very pretty or neat, but wait until you flip it over. Now you have a lovely stained glass work of art to hang in a window.

STAINED GLASS

How about super sizing your stained glass project? All you need is a piece of black butcher paper big enough to fill an entire window in your house. Cut the paper down to a size that will fit the window exactly. Divide the space up so you make 2 to 6 mini stained glass pictures inside your big piece of paper. Have fun designing your giant stained glass window.

Papier-mâché Fish

You can create wonderful bright sculptures with a cool process called *papier-mâché*. It is a French word that means "mashed paper." Strips of paper are dipped in a paste that hardens like glue. When the paper is layered over a wire shape, just about anything can be created. Papier-mâché can be messy so wear old clothes and cover your work surface!

MAKING THE FISH FORM

What you need:

- ◆ Newspapers
- ◆ Plastic bucket or bowl
- ◆ Wooden spoon
- ◆ Wire hangers
- ◆ Masking tape
- ◆ Craft paints
- ◆ Paintbrush

What you do:

1. Have an adult help you unwind the wire hanger until it is one long piece of wire. Carefully form it into the shape of a fish. To help keep the fish intact reinforce the wire with masking tape as needed.

2. Stuff the inside of the fish with wadded up pieces of newspaper. To keep the newspaper wads from falling out, reinforce with masking tape.

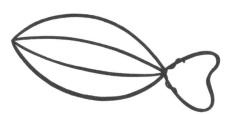

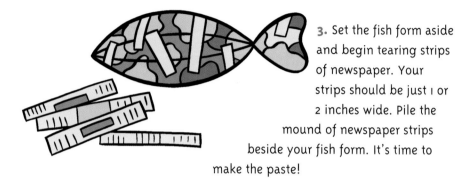

3. Set the fish form aside and begin tearing strips of newspaper. Your strips should be just 1 or 2 inches wide. Pile the mound of newspaper strips beside your fish form. It's time to make the paste!

MAKING PASTE

What you need:

- ◆ 1/2 cup flour
- ◆ 2 cups cold water
- ◆ 2 cups boiling water

1. Mix together flour and cold water in a bowl.

2. Add this mixture to the boiling water and return to a boil.

3. Remove from heat. The mixture will thicken as it cools.

4. Pour it into a big shallow dish to make it easier to dip paper.

Start your adventure:

1. Lay your fish form on a bed of layered newspaper.

2. Dip the strips of newspaper into the paste, coating them completely.

3. Place the strips carefully on the wire fish.

4. Repeat this process until the entire fish is covered with one layer of newspaper strips.

5. If it's a sunny day, leave the covered fish form outside. It will dry in 30 minutes to an hour. If left inside, it could take 1 to 2 hours. When the first layer is dry, put on a second layer of newspaper strips.

6. After your second layer is dry, you can paint your beautiful sea creature!

BRING PAPIER-MÂCHÉ TO YOUR NEXT PARTY!

Try to make a piñata (a hollow shape filled with candy) this way:

When you place paper on your wire form, leave an opening at the top about the size of a golf ball.

After your piñata is decorated, fill it with candy.

Tie a string to a Popsicle stick and insert it into the hole.

Pull the string tight, and the stick will become caught in the opening.

Have an adult help you blindfold the guests, and hold the piñata up high. Blindfolded children take turns trying to whack the piñata and break it open with a stick!

Traditionally any child who is left without a treat is given a special little basket filled with candy. This is to avoid any hurt feelings or tears.

DID YOU KNOW THIS ABOUT PIÑATAS?

Traditionally piñatas were made out of clay. People would buy the bare clay pots, take them home and paste their own color paper on them. Papier-mâché over balloons or wire structures have replaced this old tradition.

SPECTACULAR SCULPTURE

A sculpture is a work of art that can be seen from all sides. Artists can sculpt with soft clay or dough that hardens as it dries. You can buy clay at a store or make your own sculpting dough. The only other things you need are your two hands and your imagination. As you work with clay or dough, think about your sculpture from all sides because that is how everyone else will see it.

Meet An ARTIST!

Claes Oldenburg was born in 1929 in Stockholm, Sweden. In 1936, his family moved to Chicago. As a child, Claes created a entire city that he called Neuburg. He even made maps of the city, newspapers for the city, and magazines that told stories about the people who lived in his imaginary city. Claes was so full of imagination he became an artist when he grew up. In 1958, Claes started creating really yummy sculptures of hamburgers, cakes, and ice cream. His sculptures started getting bigger and bigger. In 1969, he sculpted a giant clothespin that was 45 feet high and 12 feet wide! He also sculpted a giant toothbrush, a hose, sliced peaches, pool balls, and much much more.

41

SALT DOUGH RECIPE

What you need:

4 cups flour
1 cup salt
1 ½ cups warm water

How to make salt dough:

Combine flour and salt in a bowl.

Add warm water slowly until the mixture becomes dough-like.

Knead the dough until smooth.

Cookie Cutter Mobile

What you need:
- ◆ Salt dough
- ◆ Rolling pin
- ◆ Cookie cutters in different shapes and sizes
- ◆ Spatula
- ◆ Aluminum foil
- ◆ Cookie sheet
- ◆ Craft paint
- ◆ Paintbrush
- ◆ String
- ◆ Wire hanger

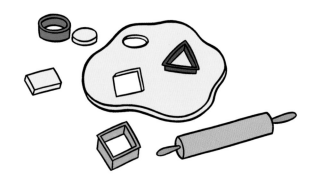

Start your adventure:

1. Sprinkle a little flour on the workspace.

2. Roll out a portion of the clay with your rolling pin. Keep rolling until the dough is about 1/2 inch thick.

3. Press your cookie cutters into the slab of dough.

4. Use the tip of a pencil to poke a hole at the top of the shapes. Make sure the hole is big enough to slide the string through.

5. With a spatula gently lift the shapes of clay onto an aluminum-covered cookie sheet.

6. Bake the cookie cutter shapes for about 30 to 45 minutes in a 350-degree oven or until hard.

7. After your creations have cooled, paint them front and back and on the sides. It's important you paint them on all sides because they will be hanging in the air and seen from all angles.

8. When the paint has dried, thread the string through the holes.

9. Tie the stringed objects to the wire hanger. Vary the lengths so they look more interesting as they dangle.

Clay Critters

There are many kinds of sculpting clay and dough that you can buy at the art supply store, or you can make your own. You can use this dough to make your own clay critters.

SCULPTING DOUGH

What you need:

4 cups flour
1 cup salt
1¾ cups warm water
Food coloring, two different colors of your choice

How to make the dough:

Mix flour, salt, and warm water in a bowl.

Knead the dough with your hands for 10 minutes. Divide the dough in half.

Add 1 drop of food coloring to one half of the dough and mix well. Add the other drop of the other color to the remaining half of dough and mix well.

Store it in a resealable container.

What you need:
- ◆ Acrylic paints
- ◆ Paintbrush
- ◆ Toothpicks
- ◆ Cheese grater and/or garlic press
- ◆ Dull table knife
- ◆ Craft Varnish

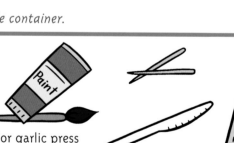

Start your art adventure:

1. Roll a piece of clay into a ball about the size of a golf ball. Make a hole in the middle with your thumb.

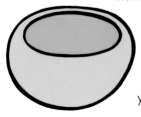

2. Pinch around and around to make a bowl. The bowl should be about ¾ inch thick. Make your critter before the bowl dries.

3. Now it's time to make your critter! Use your imagination and some handy tools to make different textures and shapes in the clay. Add whatever details you want.

CRITTER IDEAS!

Roll thin strips of dough and pinch them into tails and legs.

Roll out small balls to shape into critter heads.

Cut feathers out of thin slabs of dough.

Pinch dough into ears or wings.

Use a cheese grater or garlic press to make hair or fur.

Use toothpicks to carve texture.

Don't forget details like teeth and claws.

Mix different colors of dough to create patterns or contrast.

4. Attach the critter to the bowl. Your critter could have its arms wrapped around the bowl, or maybe it's sitting to the side of the bowl.

5. Let your sculpture air dry until it is hard, about 24 hours.

6. Paint it with acrylic paint. It can look silly or realistic.

7. After the paint has dried, have an adult help you brush on the varnish. This will help protect your critter and make it shiny.

Marvelous Masks

Did you know that masks are thought of as works of art? Artists from around the world make masks. Masks are used in parades, plays, parties and dances. Many people collect them and hang them on their walls. You can do that too!

What you need:
- ◆ Sketch paper
- ◆ Pencil or pen
- ◆ Modeling clay or self-hardening clay
- ◆ Tools to work with (try a dull knife, pizza cutter, or any other kitchen gadget that would make interesting patterns and cuts in the clay)
- ◆ Rolling pin

1. With the pencil and paper, sketch out an idea of what you want your mask to look like. Do you want to have a scary mask or a pretty one? Or how about a robot mask? The mask could even look just like you. Keep your sketch close by so you can look at it as you create your marvelous mask.

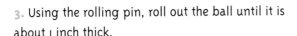

2. Start forming the clay into the size of a tennis ball. You can add or take away clay as needed.

3. Using the rolling pin, roll out the ball until it is about 1 inch thick.

4. Cut out the basic outside shape of your mask using the tools. Also cut out two eye holes, and a mouth hole if you want.

5. Make your mask come alive by adding details.

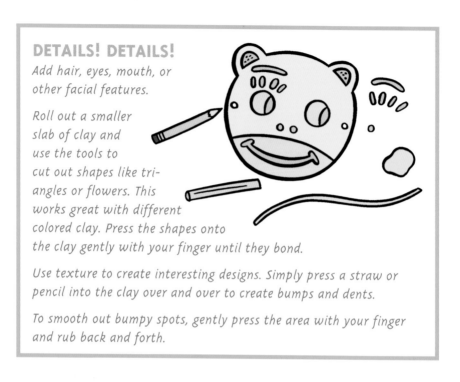

DETAILS! DETAILS!

Add hair, eyes, mouth, or other facial features.

Roll out a smaller slab of clay and use the tools to cut out shapes like triangles or flowers. This works great with different colored clay. Press the shapes onto the clay gently with your finger until they bond.

Use texture to create interesting designs. Simply press a straw or pencil into the clay over and over to create bumps and dents.

To smooth out bumpy spots, gently press the area with your finger and rub back and forth.

6. Once the mask is complete, poke two holes in the top on either side of the mask. Let the mask dry for 24 hours or until it is completely hard. If you are using baking clay, follow the instructions on the package with an adult.

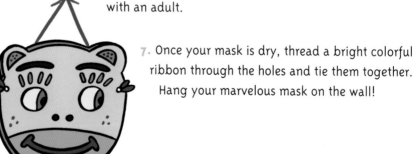

7. Once your mask is dry, thread a bright colorful ribbon through the holes and tie them together. Hang your marvelous mask on the wall!

Crazy Coil Bowls

Coils are long snakes that are rolled out of clay. When coils are placed round and round on top of another, it can make a bowl. This bowl-making style has been used for centuries to make cups, bowls, and other containers.

What you need:
- ◆ Self-hardening clay or modeling clay
- ◆ Rolling pin
- ◆ Popsicle stick
- ◆ Dull knife or toothpick

Start your art adventure:

1. Before you handle any clay, take a look at a cereal bowl. Notice how the bottom of the cereal bowl is smaller around than the top of the bowl.

2. Roll out the clay into a shape large enough to cut the bowl base out of. Use a toothpick or a dull knife. When the base is cut out, lift it up and set it aside for now.

3. To make coils, take a small amount of clay and roll it into a ball about the size of a golf ball. Gently keep rolling it, pressing a little bit harder, to make it look more like a fat snake.

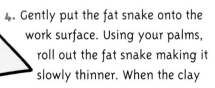

4. Gently put the fat snake onto the work surface. Using your palms, roll out the fat snake making it slowly thinner. When the clay

49

is about the same size as your pointer finger, you've made your first crazy coil!

5. Place the coil around the edge of the base and gently pat and pinch it into place.

6. Make another coil and overlap it slightly on top of the first coil. Wind it around the edge of your bowl.

7. Keep making and adding coils until the bowl looks just right. Make sure to place each coil on top of the last one.

8. Let the bowl air dry for at least 24 hours or until completely dry. If you have baking clay, follow the instructions on the package with an adult.

9. Now, your crazy coil bowl can hold anything from earrings to baseball cards.

3-D ART

Stamping paper with a carrot, using tin foil in a sculpture, and gluing your face to a clay pot! It's the kind of crazy stuff you do when you're creating 3-D art! Art that can be viewed from any angle is called "three-dimensional" or 3-D. Using rocks to paper and even garbage, artists who create 3-D art use regular materials in a different way. See what kind of art you can make using things around your house and yard.

Meet An ARTIST!

Pablo Picasso liked to experiment with art even when he was a child. He loved to paint all over the walls of his house, and one time he painted his sister with egg yolks! His parents encouraged him to pursue his dream of becoming an artist. For the rest of his life, Picasso created hundreds of paintings, drawings and sculptures. He used many ordinary things in truly unusual ways. Picasso even invented many new art techniques, such as the collage.

Veggie Greeting Cards

What you need:

◆ Vegetables, such as red peppers, cabbage, mushrooms, or onions
◆ Craft paint
◆ Plain white greeting cards or folded card-sized pieces of white paper
◆ Paper or plastic plates
◆ Paintbrush

Start your art adventure:

1. Cut all of the vegetables in half.

2. Squeeze your paint colors onto the plates. You can usually fit two colors per plate.

3. Dip one of the vegetable halves in the paint. Make sure it doesn't have too much paint on it. Use your brush to wipe away any excess.

4. Stamp the veggie on your card. Overlap your different veggie stamps, and use lots of bright colors. Stamp the outside of the envelope too!

VEGGIE STAMPS

You can use more than just veggies to make a stamp. Go on a treasure hunt and look for objects that have an interesting pattern and feel to them. Try to find these things:

An old shoe

A leaf

A packing peanut

A piece of old carpet

A scrunched up piece of tinfoil or plastic wrap

Your foot or hand

All these objects make great stamps. Use a sponge to apply the paint—it's easier.

Stick Painting

◆ Natural sticks of all sizes
◆ Rag
◆ Acrylic or craft paints
◆ Clear acrylic glaze
◆ Paper or plastic plates
◆ Paintbrushes

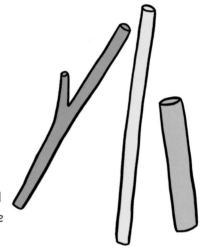

Start your art adventure:

1. Gather the sticks. Look for sticks that have little or no bark, as they will be easier to paint. Also, the bigger the stick the easier it will be to paint.

2. Get the sticks ready to paint by stripping off any excess bark and dusting them with a rag.

3. Paint the entire stick one color. White, black, or dark blue are great choices.

4. After it has dried, paint designs of all sorts on your stick. Pick a theme for your stick. Do you love stripes, soccer, polka dots, or hearts? These could all be possible themes for your stick.

5. When you have finished, spray the painted stick with a clear acrylic glaze. The glaze will make it shiny and help to protect it.

WHAT CAN I DO WITH MY STICK?

Hang your stick horizontally on a wall.

If it is sturdy enough, use it as a walking stick.

Nail two sticks together to form a cross, then hang a mobile from them.

Push one end of your stick in a flower bed for an outdoor decoration, or group several painted sticks together.

Place one end into the dirt of a house-plant for a cheery addition.

Tie old silverware or other clinky-clanky objects to it to form a wind chime.

Pieces of You

What you need:

- ◆ Old magazines
- ◆ White glue or glue stick
- ◆ Heavy paper or poster board
- ◆ Brush for gluing
- ◆ Scissors
- ◆ Small objects with interesting shapes like dry pasta, leaves, or paper clips
- ◆ Any personal objects like charms, award ribbons, old sheet music, or report cards

Start your art adventure:

1. Look through the magazines and cut out pictures that are all about you— foods, hobbies, colors, people, words, sports, cars—all your favorites.

2. Arrange the pictures in a collage-like fashion on your paper. Remember, in a collage you can overlap things.

3. Add the interesting objects to your collage. Make shapes or frames, or just fill in empty spaces. Add the personal objects also, as long as they can be glued on easily.

4. This collage is all about you, so have fun!

CRACK 'EM UP CARDS!

Make funny collage cards for your family and friends. Cut out pictures in magazines and then combine them. For example, try putting a dog's head on a human body! Or placing butterfly wings on an apple. Mix and match unusual images and glue them on a card to get a laugh.

What a Relief Sculpture

A relief sculpture is a work of art where details stand out from the background.

What you need:

- 12" x 12" piece of cardboard
- Aluminum foil
- Scissors
- White glue
- Pencils
- Paintbrushes
- A handful of objects with interesting shapes, like leaves, twigs, sea shells, plastic forks, paper clips, or feathers
- Yarn or string
- Black or dark acrylic paint
- Cloth or paper towels

Start your adventure:

1. Cut aluminum foil 2 inches larger than your piece of cardboard on all sides. Set the foil aside for now.

2. Use glue to adhere the interesting objects to the cardboard square. Remember to have a variety of sizes, shapes, and texture.

3. Lightly brush glue over all of the objects and cardboard.

4. Have an adult help you cover your cardboard with foil, but don't tuck the edges behind the cardboard yet.

5. Gently press the foil over and around your objects beginning in the center. Use the rounded end of a paintbrush to carefully press it around the edges of your objects. Use a stiff paintbrush to press the foil into the textures of the different objects. Be careful you don't poke a hole in the foil.

6. Fold the edges neatly behind the cardboard and glue a string hanger to the back.

7. To make your sculpture awesome, water down the acrylic paints and brush it over your entire foil image! Immediately wipe it with a damp soft cloth or paper towel. The raised areas should shine.

What a relief! You've finished your relief sculpture. Hang it where you can enjoy it every day.

Pot of Photos

Have you ever wanted to smear glue all over your brother or sister's face? In this project, you can! This project lets you choose your favorite photos and keep them forever on a flower pot.

What you need:

◆ Clay pot
◆ Newspapers
◆ Mod Podge (from a craft store) or glue that dries clear
◆ Colored copies of your favorite photos
◆ Craft paints
◆ Brush for gluing
◆ Brushes for paints

Start your art adventure:

1. Set your clay pot on top of the layered newspaper.

2. Brush the back of each photo copy with glue or Mod Podge and place them on your pot. You can overlap the photos or glue them on at different angles.

3. Paint little designs on the empty places of your pot. You could even write pretty words or the names of your family members in the empty spots.

4. After the paint has dried, brush a coat of Mod Podge over the entire pot.

5. Fill your pot with flowers or pencils and pens.

GLUE WHO?

Here are some items that would make great surfaces for a picture collage:

An old table

A scrapbook cover

A picture frame

A washed out yogurt container

A shoe box to store your photos

Remember to ask permission before starting any of these photo adventures!

GLOSSARY

Charcoal—A black, porous, drawing instrument.

Collage—Pasting different materials onto a surface to creating art.

Contour—The simple outline of an object.

Impression—A mark made on a surface by pressure.

Mosaic—A design made by setting small colored pieces, such as stone or tile, into a surface.

Negative space—The empty space around an object.

Papier-mâché—A sculpture made from strips of paper mixed with glue or paste that can be molded into various shapes when wet and becomes hard when dry.

Positive space—Space that an object fills up.

Radial—Designs coming out from a common center.

Relief—The projection of objects from a flat background, as in sculpture.

Silhouette—An outline of something that is filled in with a solid color.

Symmetrical—Something that is equal on all sides.

Texture—The appearance and feel of a surface.

WEBSITES TO VISIT

http://www.colormatters.com/entercolormatters.html (all about color)

http://www.kidsart.com/topten.html (links to lots of kid's art pages)

http://www.nga.gov/kids/ (National Gallery of Art)

http://www.si.edu/kids/ (Smithsonian Museum website for kids)

http://www.ibiblio.org/wm/paint/auth/gogh/ (Van Gogh)

http://en.wikipedia.org/wiki/Picasso (Picasso)

http://dmoz.org/Kids_and_Teens/People_and_Society/Biography/Artists/Matisse,_Henri/ (Matisse)

http://www.oldenburgvanbruggen.com/lsp.htm (Oldenburg)

http://www.factmonster.com/ (tips for all artists)

http://www.nationalgeographic.com/kids/index.html (make cartoons)

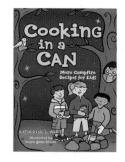